Sports Illustrated **KIDS**

GAME-CHANGING COACHES

FOOTBALL'S BEST
COACHES

Influencers, Leaders, and Winners on the Field

written by Mari Bolte

CAPSTONE PRESS
a capstone imprint

Published by Capstone Press, an imprint of Capstone
1710 Roe Crest Drive, North Mankato, Minnesota 56003
capstonepub.com

SPORTS ILLUSTRATED KIDS is a trademark of ABG-SI LLC. Used with permission.

Library of Congress Cataloging-in-Publication Data
Names: Bolte, Mari, author.
Title: Football's best coaches : influencers, leaders, and winners on the field / by Mari Bolte.
Description: North Mankato, Minnesota : Capstone Press, [2024] | Series: Sports illustrated kids: game-changing coaches | Includes bibliographical references and index. | Audience: Ages 8-11 | Audience: Grades 4-6 | Summary: "The players aren't the only stars on the football field. Football's most influential college and professional coaches are stars in their own right. Which coaches have the longest winning streaks? Who has coached the most championship winners. And which coaches have changed the game as we know it? Turn these pages to find out!"— Provided by publisher.
Identifiers: LCCN 2023021246 (print) | LCCN 2023021247 (ebook) | ISBN 9781669063469 (hardcover) | ISBN 9781669063810 (paperback) | ISBN 9781669063506 (pdf) | ISBN 9781669063544 (epub) | ISBN 9781669063551 (kindle edition)
Subjects: LCSH: Football coaches—United States—Juvenile literature. | Football—Coaching—United States—Juvenile literature. | Football coaches—Rating of—United States—Juvenile literature.
Classification: LCC GV939.A1 B65 2024 (print) | LCC GV939.A1 (ebook) | DDC 796.332092/2—dc23/eng/20230503
LC record available at https://lccn.loc.gov/2023021246
LC ebook record available at https://lccn.loc.gov/2023021247

Editorial Credits
Editor: Mandy Robbins; Designer: Dina Her; Media Researcher: Jo Miller; Production Specialist: Tori Abraham

Image Credits
Associated Press: David Durochik, 19, Pro Football Hall of Fame, 14, Robert Klein, 16, St. Cloud Times, Dave Schwarz, 8, Stephen Morton, File, 10; Getty Images: Focus on Sport, 25, GeorgePeters, design element (throughout), Library of Congress, 26, Rob Carr, 17, Sporting News Archive, 23, Stephen Dunn, 15, traffic_analyzer, Cover (top left), Yale University/Handout, 13; Shutterstock: enterlinedesign, Cover (middle), inspiring.team, Cover, design element, Milano M, design element (throughout), Mtsaride, Cover (bottom right), Tusumaru, background (throughout); Sports Illustrated: Al Tielemans, Cover (bottom left), 21, 28, Erick W. Rasco, 11, John Iacono, 18, John W. McDonough, 22, Neil Leifer, Cover (top right), 7, 27, Simon Bruty, 9, Walter Iooss Jr., 5

Printed and bound in the USA. 5626

TABLE OF CONTENTS

Words in **BOLD** are in the glossary.

INTRODUCTION

THE VALUE OF A GOOD COACH

An impossible catch. A hail-Mary touchdown throw. A game-changing turnover. Exciting moments like these draw people to watch their favorite football teams. But the athletes on the field aren't the only ones behind those amazing plays.

A good coach is just as important as an **elite** quarterback. The very best coaches go down in history. The things they bring to the sport live on long after they **retire**. Some came up with new ideas that made football better. Others set records that still stand today. These game-changing coaches made impacts that will never be forgotten.

CHAPTER 1
HOOKED ON WINNING

Some people start out their careers winning and never look back. These coaches have won more games than most people will watch over an entire lifetime.

Don Shula played pro ball before he coached. In 1963, the Baltimore Colts hired him as their head coach. He moved to the Miami Dolphins in 1970. The Dolphins went on to win more than 10 games every season. The 1972–73 team was undefeated. Their Super Bowl victory gave them a perfect season. This feat has yet to be repeated. Despite his perfect season, Shula never felt like he was done learning.

"I never felt I knew it all. I always felt there's something new to learn, something new to do."
—Don Shula

Shula (right) talks with his quarterback, Bob Griese, during the 1972 playoffs.

Shula was a head coach for 33 seasons. His record is 347 wins, 173 losses, and 6 ties. Under his leadership, the Dolphins went to the Super Bowl six times. They won twice.

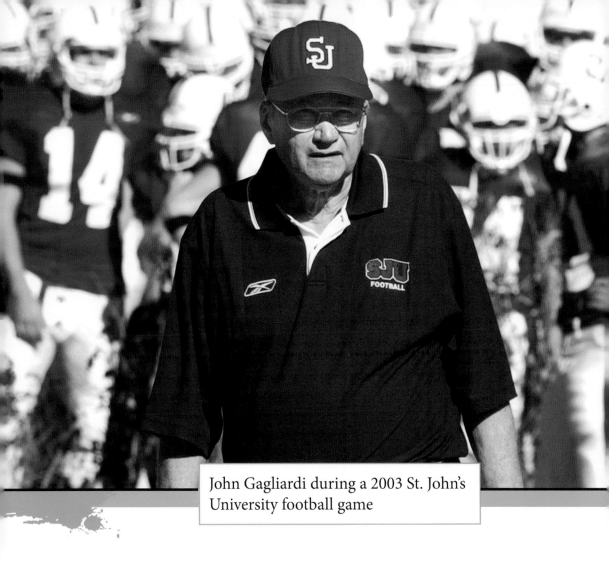

John Gagliardi during a 2003 St. John's University football game

John Gagliardi made college football his life. He coached for 64 years. Sixty of those seasons were at St. John's University in Collegeville, Minnesota. With a record of 489 wins, 138 losses, and 11 ties, he is the winningest coach in college football. In 2006, Gagliardi became the first active coach to be **inducted** into the College Football **Hall of Fame**. He did not retire until 2012.

In 1991, the Cleveland Browns were coming off a depressing 3–13 season. They hired Bill Belichick to turn things around. By 1994, the Browns were 11–5.

In 2000, Belichick joined the New England Patriots. Under his leadership, they won the Super Bowl six times. By the end of the 2022 season, Belichick had 329 career wins—second only to Don Shula. Belichick formed a tight bond with quarterback Tom Brady. Even after Brady left the Patriots, he praised his former coach.

"He's been an amazing coach that I got to play for for 20 years . . . He works incredibly hard, and he's incredibly deserving of all the accolades that go along with it."
—Tom Brady

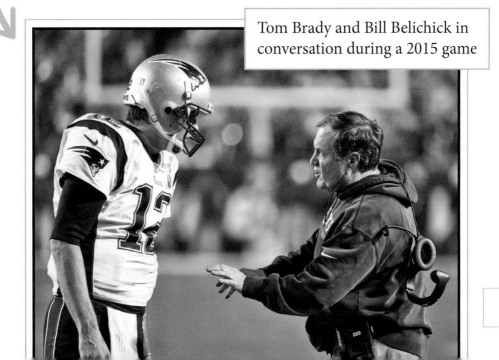

Tom Brady and Bill Belichick in conversation during a 2015 game

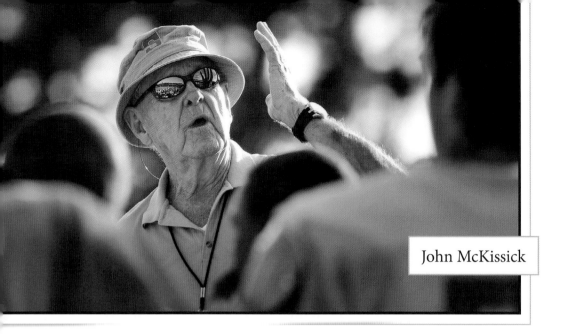

John McKissick

John McKissick is known as the winningest coach in America. He coached at Summerville High School in South Carolina. His record of 621 wins, 155 losses, and 13 ties includes 10 state championships. McKissick coached at Summerville for 63 years. Only two of those seasons were losing years. The team went undefeated five times. In 2012, McKissick became the first American football coach in history—at any level—to reach 600 victories.

Fact

There are 32 teams in the National Football League (NFL). There are way more collegiate teams—834!

Knute Rockne was born in Norway, but he made America his home. He attended college and played football for the University of Notre Dame in South Bend, Indiana. He was hired as the head coach there in 1918. Notre Dame's overall record under Rockne was 105 wins, 12 losses, and 5 ties. His winning percentage of .881 is the highest in college history.

A statue of Knute Rockne stands outside Notre Dame Stadium.

KNUTE ROCKNE
HEAD COACH
1918 — 1930
105 WINS, 12 LOSSES, 5 TIES
NATIONAL CHAMPIONS: 1924, 1929, 1930

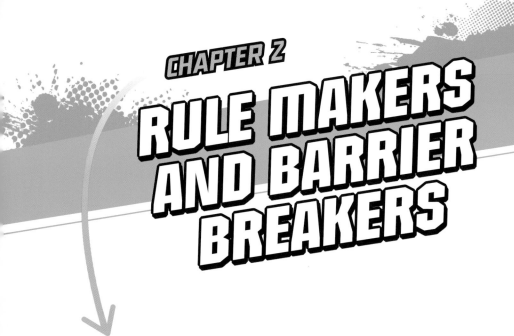

CHAPTER 2
RULE MAKERS AND BARRIER BREAKERS

Games have rules. But those rules are made to be rewritten! Changes can make the game safer, more exciting, and more inclusive. These coaches brought fresh ideas to the game that are still used today.

Walter Camp is known as the Father of American Football. Camp played for Yale University. The college hired him to coach in 1888. Camp had a new idea. He used pictures to show his players what he wanted them to do. He also created the **down** system and the **line of scrimmage**. In 1891, he published *American Football*. It was the first book about football ever written.

Walter Camp, 1920

Fact

American football is related to rugby. Established in 1869, it was originally a game of running and kicking. Passing was later added to make the game less violent.

Glenn Scobey "Pop" Warner was hired at the Carlisle Indian Industrial School in Pennsylvania in 1899. The **indigenous** players on his team were fast. However, they were also much smaller than the teams they faced. Warner came up with trick plays. The "Carlisle formation" let his players run, pass, or kick. They also used forward passes. These moves kept the ball away from larger, slower defenses.

Warner (right) instructs his players.

In 1941, Grambling State University, a historically black college in Louisiana, hired Eddie Robinson to coach. Robinson and his team traveled across America. He showed that Black players could play as well as white players. Black players didn't play in the NFL from 1934 to 1946 due to racism. During Robinson's 57 seasons, more than 200 of his players went pro.

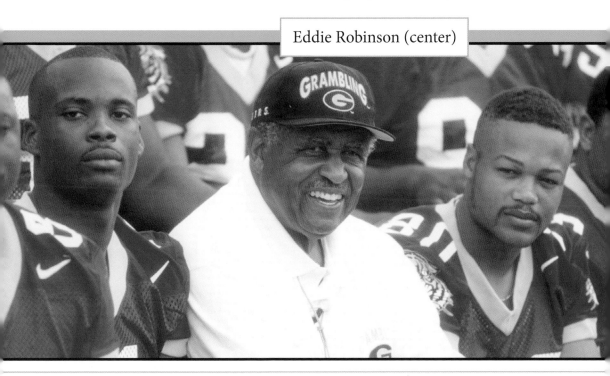

Eddie Robinson (center)

Fact

Robinson made sure his players were well dressed and well behaved. They were expected to wear suits and ties. He even gave them **etiquette** lessons!

Al Davis (center), 1963

Al Davis served as the head coach of the Oakland Raiders for much of the 1960s. He was also the team's general manager and the principle owner. Davis was a leader on and off the field. He would not let his team play in cities where players were **segregated**. He hired the NFL's first Black head coach in Art Shell and second Latino head coach in Tom Flores. In 1997, he hired Amy Trask. She was the NFL's first female CEO.

Women in the Field

There are no female head coaches in the NFL—yet. But there are plenty of other women paving the way! In 2015, Jen Welter joined the league. She was the linebacker coach for the Arizona Cardinals. Offensive assistant coach Katie Sowers was the first woman and openly gay coach in a Super Bowl. She went there with the San Francisco 49ers in 2020. In 2022, the Raiders hired Sandra Douglass Morgan as their new team president. She is the first Black woman in this role. In 2022, Autumn Lockwood was hired as an assistant performance coach for the Philadelphia Eagles. In 2023, she became the first Black woman to coach in a Super Bowl.

Autumn Lockwood speaks with Josh Jobe during a 2023 practice.

The San Francisco 49ers hired Bill Walsh to lead the team in 1979. He had been an assistant coach for the Cincinnati Bengals. There, he had tested out a new idea. It would become known as the "West Coast Offense." It changed the game of football from tackling and collisions to a thinking game.

Bill Walsh addresses quarterback Joe Montana during a 1982 game.

What's West Coast Offense?

Walsh's West Coast Offense included new ways to move the football down the field. Previously, the quarterback would run forward when the ball was snapped. But Walsh had his quarterback drop back three or five steps instead. This gave receivers time to run in different patterns. The quarterback would look at where the defensive players were. Then he could throw the ball to an open receiver.

Bengals quarterback Ken Anderson drops back for a pass in 1981 game.

CHAPTER 3

WINNING AT BOTH LEVELS

Going pro is something players and coaches dream of. But college coaches don't move up to the NFL as often as you might think. Between 2000 and 2021, only 11 coaches made the move. Other coaches have moved from the pros to the college level. Being successful at both levels is a big challenge. These coaches made their mark on college and pro players.

Nick Saban has coached briefly at the pro level, but he's known as the greatest coach in collegiate football history. Saban has coached his teams to a record seven NCAA Division One National Championships. His first was at Louisiana State University in 2004. He has coached the Alabama Crimson Tide since 2007. They have won six national collegiate titles together.

Nick Saban gets heated during a 2012 game.

Fact

As of 2022, Alabama had 58 former players in the NFL.

Only three coaches have won both a Super Bowl and a college football national championship. Pete Carroll is one of them. From 2001 to 2009, Carroll coached the University of Southern California Trojans. They had six bowl game wins and back-to-back national championships. Carroll also coached the Seattle Seahawks to two Super Bowls. They won once. Carroll often looked for underrated players and coached them to success.

"Coach Carroll, he's unorthodox in his approach. He actually looks for guys that other people might not think are very good, or might not fit their idea of a particular defense. He uses it to his benefit."
—Seattle defensive end Red Bryant

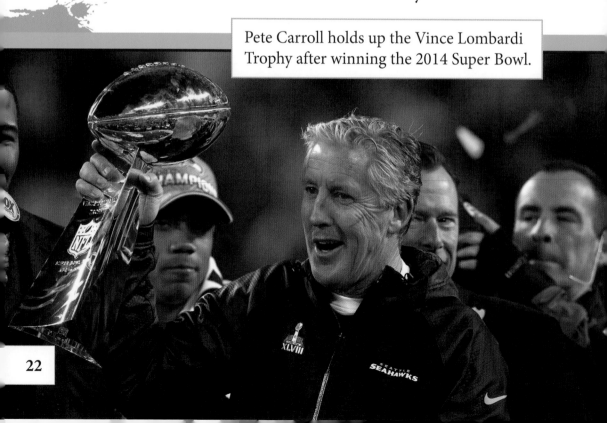

Pete Carroll holds up the Vince Lombardi Trophy after winning the 2014 Super Bowl.

Alfred Earle "Greasy" Neale played pro baseball while also coaching college football. His team at Washington and Jefferson College went to the 1922 Rose Bowl. It was the only Rose Bowl to end in a scoreless tie. In 1941, Neale became the head coach for the Philadelphia Eagles. They won the NFL Championship in 1948 and 1949. Neale was the first coach to be inducted into to both the College and Pro Football Halls of Fame.

Alfred Earle "Greasy" Neale, 1940s

CHAPTER 4
WINNING STREAKS

It's one thing to win a bowl game, a championship, or a Super Bowl. It's another to keep on winning. These coaches proved their success wasn't just a fluke.

The name Vince Lombardi goes hand in hand with football. His first year as the head coach of the Green Bay Packers was in 1959. That same season, he was named the NFL Coach of the Year. The Packers won the first two Super Bowls under Lombardi's leadership. Lombardi never had a losing season with the Packers. Since 1970, the Rotary Lombardi Award has been given to the nation's best collegiate lineman. And in 1971, the Super Bowl trophy was renamed the Vince Lombardi Trophy in his honor.

Lombardi had a way with words. Many of his motivational quotes continue to inspire athletes today.

Lombardi's players carry him off the field after winning the Super Bowl in 1967.

"The only place 'success' comes before 'work' is in the dictionary."
—Vince Lombardi

Amos Alonzo Stagg coached the University of Chicago Maroons. His record was 227 wins, 112 losses, and 26 ties. The Maroons won seven Big Ten Conference championships. Stagg's career lasted a record 71 years. He also coached track, baseball, and basketball. The College Football Hall of Fame added him as both a player and a coach in 1951.

Stagg didn't just coach to win. He wanted to help young men develop into good human beings. He was asked after winning the college football national championship what he thought of his team. He replied, "I'll let you know in 20 years."

Amos Alonzo Stagg (center) speaking to players

Bryant on the sidelines during a 1974 game

Until 2020, Bear Bryant held the record for the most collegiate victories. Bryant took 29 college teams to bowl games. Fifteen of those led to conference championships. As Alabama's coach, he earned six national titles. He coached until the end. He died on January 26, 1983. That was just 28 days after his final game—which, of course, he won.

Mike Tomlin became the Pittsburgh Steelers head coach in 2007. He was only the third head coach hired to the team since 1969. By his second year, the Steelers won the Super Bowl! Tomlin was only 36 at the time. He was the youngest person to coach a Super Bowl-winning team. In 2023, he hit another milestone. He became the first coach in NFL history to have 16 straight non-losing seasons.

Coaches are the planners, the leaders, and the brains behind the team. Thanks to game-changing coaches throughout history, football has become more fun and exciting than ever.

Fact

At one point in 2022, Tomlin was the only Black head coach in the NFL. So far, there have been more than 500 NFL head coaches. Between 2012 and 2021, only 11 were people of color.

TIMELINE

1891   *American Football* comes out. Written by Walter Camp, it is the first book about football ever published.

1918   Knute Rockne is hired as the head coach of the University of Notre Dame.

1941   Eddie Robinson is hired to coach at Grambling State University.

1951   Amos Alonzo Stagg is inducted into the College Football Hall of Fame as both a coach and a player.

1966   Former coach and general manager Al Davis becomes principle owner of the Oakland Raiders.

1970   The Super Bowl trophy is formally renamed the Vince Lombardi Trophy. It is first awarded to the Baltimore Colts in 1971.

1973   Don Shula's Miami Dolphins finish an undefeated season and come home with a Super Bowl victory.

1979   Bill Walsh brings the West Coast Offense to the San Francisco 49ers.

1983   Bear Bryant retires with 323 collegiate victories.

2000   Bill Belichick begins his career with the New England Patriots.

2007   Nick Saban begins coaching at the University of Alabama.

2012   John Gagliardi retires after coaching for 64 years.

2012   John McKissick earns his 600th win.

2014   Pete Carroll leads the Seattle Seahawks to their first Super Bowl win.

2023   Mike Tomlin ends the season as the only NFL coach with 16 non-losing seasons in a row.

GLOSSARY

DOWN (DOWN)—a play in football; a team gets four downs, or chances, to move the football forward 10 yards

ELITE (i-LEET)—describes players who are among the best in the league

ETIQUETTE (ET-uh-kuht)—the practice of good manners in social situations

HALL OF FAME (HALL OF FAYM)—a place where important people are honored

INDIGENOUS (in-DID-juh-nuss)—native to a place

INDUCT (in-DUHKT)—to formally admit someone into a position or place of honor

LINE OF SCRIMMAGE (LINE UHV SKRIM-ij)—the imaginary line running across the width of a football field; each play beings at the line of scrimmage

RETIRE (ri-TIRE)—to give up a line of work

SEGREGATED (SEG-ruh-gay-ted)—separated by race

READ MORE

Anderson, Josh. *Inside the Seattle Seahawks*. Minneapolis: Lerner Publications, 2024.

Berglund, Bruce. *Football Records Smashed!* North Mankato, MN: Capstone Press, 2024.

Coleman, Ted. *Las Vegas Raiders*. Mendota Heights, MN: Press Room Editions, 2021.

INTERNET SITES

Britannica Kids: Football
kids.britannica.com/kids/article/football/353142

DK Find Out! Football
dkfindout.com/us/sports/football/

Ranking the 50 Best NFL Head Coaches of All Time
bleacherreport.com/articles/1168549-ranking-the-50-best-nfl-head-coaches-of-all-time

INDEX

ABOUT THE AUTHOR

Mari Bolte is the author and editor of many books for children, ranging from video games to cute animals to sports stars. A lifelong Green Bay Packers fan, she lives in the frozen tundra and dreams of Lambeau leaps.